EXPLORE THE WORLD

THE GEOGRAPHY OF LATIN AMERICA

KATE MIKOLEY

PowerKiDS press

New York

Published in 2021 by The Rosen Publishing Group, Inc.
29 East 21st Street, New York, NY 10010

First Edition

Editor: Caitie McAneney
Book Design: Tanya Dellaccio

Photo Credits: Cover Pawel Krupinski Photography/Moment/Getty Images; series background MicroOne/Shutterstock.com; p. 5 https://upload.wikimedia.org/wikipedia/commons/6/62/Latin_America_regions.svg; p. 7 (top) FernandoPodolski/E+/Getty Images; p. 7 (bottom) sunsinger/Shutterstock.com; p. 9 (both) Victor Moriyama/Getty Images News/Getty Images; p. 11 Jess Kraft/Shutterstock.com; p. 13 Gerard Prins/Moment Open/Getty Images; p. 14 Olga Kot Photo/Shutterstock.com; p. 15 Go Ga/500px Prime/Getty Images; p. 17 J.Castro/Moment/Getty Images; p. 19 Alex Cimbal/Shutterstock.com; p. 21 (top) ivanastar/E+/Getty Images; p. 21 (bottom) Rainer Lesniewski/Shutterstock.com; p. 23 pingebat/Shutterstock.com; p. 25 (both) ALFREDO ESTRELLA/AFP/Getty Images; p. 27 Gerard Ruiters/Moment/Getty Images; p. 29 (top) Adwo/Shutterstock.com; p. 29 (bottom) Gustavo Frazao/Shutterstock.com.

Cataloging-in-Publication Data
Names: Mikoley, Kate.
Title: The geography of Latin America / Kate Mikoley.
Description: New York : PowerKids Press, 2021. | Series: Explore the world | Includes glossary and index.
Identifiers: ISBN 9781725321922 (pbk.) | ISBN 9781725321946 (library bound) | ISBN 9781725321939 (6 pack) | ISBN 9781725321953 (ebook)
Subjects: LCSH: Latin America–Juvenile literature. | Physical geography–Latin America–Juvenile literature. | Latin America–Geography–Juvenile literature.
Classification: LCC GB458.9 M63 2020 | DDC 918.02–dc23

Manufactured in the United States of America

CPSIA Compliance Information: Batch #CSPK20: For Further Information contact Rosen Publishing, New York, New York at 1-800-237-9932

Find us on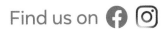

CONTENTS

LET'S LOOK AT LATIN AMERICA

From the cactus-dotted desert of northern Mexico all the way to the Patagonian ice fields of Argentina lies a group of countries we call Latin America. Most people in these countries speak a language that comes from Latin, the language of ancient Rome. These languages are often referred to as Romance languages. Common Romance languages spoken in Latin America today are Spanish and Portuguese, as well as French.

At the northernmost part of Latin America is the country of Mexico. Below that is Central America, which includes the countries of Belize, Guatemala, Honduras, El Salvador, Nicaragua, Costa Rica, and Panama. All of the countries on the continent of South America are also part of Latin America, as well as islands in the Caribbean where people speak a Romance language, such as Puerto Rico and Haiti.

THE PEOPLES OF LATIN AMERICA

Beginning in the late 1400s, many parts of Latin America were **colonized** by the people of Spain and Portugal, who brought their languages and their religion, Catholicism. Many people in this region still speak Spanish and Portuguese today. Europeans also brought slaves from Africa to this area to work. Colonization and slavery affected the **demography** in Latin America. In colonial times, a social class structure gave more power to Europeans and people of mixed European descent than it gave to people with purely **indigenous** or African roots. Today, Latin America has a very diverse, or varied, population.

Countries in Latin America may share a history of colonization by the Spanish and Portuguese, but they're all unique places—especially when it comes to their geography and landforms.

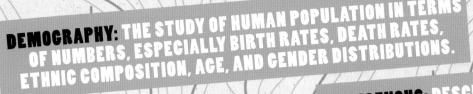

- ■ **NORTH AMERICA**
- ■ **CARIBBEAN**
- ■ **CENTRAL AMERICA**
- ■ **SOUTH AMERICA**

THINK LIKE A GEOGRAPHER

LATIN AMERICA IS OFTEN BROKEN INTO FOUR SMALLER REGIONS, OR SUBREGIONS. THESE ARE NORTH AMERICA [MEXICO], SOUTH AMERICA, CENTRAL AMERICA, AND THE CARIBBEAN.

INTO THE AMAZON

Brazil is the largest country in Latin America. It's located in central and eastern South America, where it takes up about half the space of all the land. If you were to travel from the top of the country to the bottom, you'd cover around 2,700 miles (4,345.2 km). However, you'd likely hit some rough **terrain** along the way, including wetlands, **savannas**, and the Amazon River **basin**.

The Amazon River stretches nearly 4,000 miles (6,437.4 km) across South America. Measured by volume, it's the largest river in the world, beginning in Peru and flowing into the Atlantic Ocean at Brazil's northeast coast. Affecting much of South America's geography, its enormous basin is home to more than 1,000 **tributaries** and the Amazon Rain Forest.

THINK LIKE A GEOGRAPHER

BRAZIL IS THE FIFTH LARGEST COUNTRY IN THE WORLD BY AREA, AFTER RUSSIA, CANADA, CHINA, AND THE UNITED STATES. ITS FORMER CAPITAL CITY, RIO DE JANEIRO, HOSTED THE 2016 SUMMER OLYMPICS.

BASIN: A LARGE AREA OF LAND THAT IS LOWER THAN THE AREA AROUND IT.

Manatees in the Amazon migrate, or move to other areas, depending on how much rain falls.

LIFE IN THE AMAZON

The Amazon Rain Forest takes up about 40 percent of Brazil's area. It's home to millions of species of animals, plants, and other organisms. From tiny insects to the world's largest living rodent, the capybara, the Amazon supports many kinds of life. There are even manatees living in the Amazon River. The rain forest is so large and varied that people haven't even discovered all of the organisms that live there. Perhaps more Amazonian species will be discovered in your lifetime!

CAPYBARA

DEFORESTATION IN THE AMAZON

Many people consider the Amazon Rain Forest to be one of the most beautiful places in the world, but sadly, it has been getting smaller. **Climate change** and human actions have greatly harmed this region.

As Brazil's population grew in the 1900s, more space was needed for people to live. With the Amazon taking up so much of Brazil's area, it made sense that people started moving into parts of the country once occupied by the rain forest. As people started to move in, they cleared trees to make room for new homes, farms, and ranches. They also cut down trees to be used for lumber, or material for building. This act of clearing forests to be used for other purposes is called deforestation.

THINK LIKE A GEOGRAPHER

DEFORESTATION DESTROYS TREES AND OTHER PLANT LIFE IN A FOREST. IT ALSO RUINS HABITATS NECESSARY FOR NATIVE ANIMALS.

In 2019, around 75,000 fires burned through the Amazon Rain Forest. Fires are not uncommon in the Amazon, but they're usually worse in dry years. That year was not especially dry, so the high amount of fires was troubling.

HELPING THE RAIN FOREST

By 2016, about 80 percent of what had been covered by the Amazon Rain Forest in 1970 was still there. However, the rate at which it was shrinking had slowed. In the 1990s, the government of Brazil took measures to reduce deforestation and other threats to the rain forest. In the 1980s and 1990s, about 0.4 percent of the forest was lost each year. Only about 0.2 percent was lost each year between 2008 and 2016.

CHANGING THE ECOSYSTEM

In addition to Brazil, the Amazon covers parts of Peru, Colombia, and several other countries. As wildfires burn and other forms of deforestation worsen, **significant** changes are happening in the forest's ecosystems.

The Amazon Rain Forest is responsible for much of the rain that falls in South America. If it's destroyed, the continent would likely become much hotter and drier. This could destroy agricultural areas that the Amazon has previously been able to support and seriously decrease **natural resources**. Additionally, it's possible that this change in the climate would make it so certain organisms—including humans—could not live in parts of South America where they currently **thrive**. But it wouldn't just be South America—rainfall on other continents would likely be affected as well.

THE AMAZON AND CLIMATE CHANGE

The Amazon is an important resource for the entire world, not just Latin America. Its soil and plant life take in around 5 percent of the carbon dioxide that the world emits, or gives off, every year. This helps fight climate change. If the rain forest continues burning and losing forest area, it could start releasing the carbon dioxide it has been storing. This could be as harmful as five years' worth of **fossil fuels** emitted around the world.

If rainfall decreases in the Amazon, it could make areas in other parts of Latin America that are currently **arable** unable to support agriculture and human life.

THINK LIKE A GEOGRAPHER

SOME SCIENTISTS ESTIMATED IN 2019 THAT IF ANOTHER 10 PERCENT OF THE AMAZON IS DESTROYED, IT WOULD BECOME SO DRY THAT IT WOULD NO LONGER BE CONSIDERED A RAIN FOREST. IT WOULD BECOME A SAVANNA.

ATACAMA DESERT

It may seem surprising that the continent that holds the Amazon Rain Forest is also home to the world's driest place—the Atacama Desert. It's true, though—from mountains and plains to rivers and deserts, the geography of South America is incredibly varied.

Located in northern Chile to the west of the Andes Mountains, the Atacama Desert averages only about 0.04 inch (0.1 cm) of rain each year. In some parts of the desert, no amount of rain has ever been recorded! The severe dryness makes for tough conditions for organisms to survive in. Very few plants and animals have the adaptations required to live here. Even bacteria and insects have trouble adapting to the harsh climate of the Atacama Desert.

THINK LIKE A GEOGRAPHER

A USEFUL RESOURCE FOUND IN THE ATACAMA DESERT IS A CHEMICAL COMPOUND CALLED SODIUM NITRATE. ONE OF ITS MANY USES IS AS A FERTILIZER.

MINE FULL OF COPPER

Though most plants and animals can't survive in the Atacama Desert, at least one valuable resource is found here—copper. A reddish-brown metal found in the earth, copper is a huge source of income for Chile's economy. Many people work mining, or digging, copper in areas where the element's supply is rich. The Escondida Mine, located in the Atacama Desert, is one of the highest-producing copper mines in the world.

In Spanish, *escondida* means "hidden." For years, the copper near the Escondida Mine was hidden deep below Earth's surface.

THE AMAZING ANDES

Latin America has the longest chain of mountain ranges in the world—the Andes. These mountains span about 4,500 miles (7,242 km) along the western coast of South America and go through seven Latin American countries: Argentina, Bolivia, Chile, Colombia, Ecuador, Peru, and Venezuela. The Andes act as a barrier between the Pacific Ocean and the part of South America to the east of the mountains. This affects the climate of much of the continent and makes for quite different weather patterns on the western and eastern sides of the mountains.

The highest peak in the Western Hemisphere, Mount Aconcagua, sits along the border of Argentina and Chile in the Andes. High **altitudes** have lower oxygen levels, which makes it difficult to breathe in some parts of the Andes.

THINK LIKE A GEOGRAPHER

LAKE TITICACA, LOCATED IN THE ANDES MOUNTAINS ALONG THE BORDER OF PERU AND BOLIVIA, IS THE WORLD'S HIGHEST BODY OF WATER THAT LARGE SHIPS CAN NAVIGATE.

ELEVATION: HEIGHT ABOVE SEA LEVEL.

LIFE IN THE MOUNTAINS

While many cities can be found around the Andes, the low oxygen level near the higher peaks makes it tough for humans to live there. Over time, however, some shepherds in Peru have adapted to the **elevation** and are able to live in places above 17,000 feet [5,181.6 m]! Elevations higher than 12,000 feet [3,657.6 m] have such little oxygen that people whose families have lived there for a long time have a different cell makeup than people who live at lower elevations!

In the 1400s, the Incas lived in Machu Picchu, an area tourists now visit to see Incan ruins at about 7,710 feet [2,350 m] up in Peru's Andes.

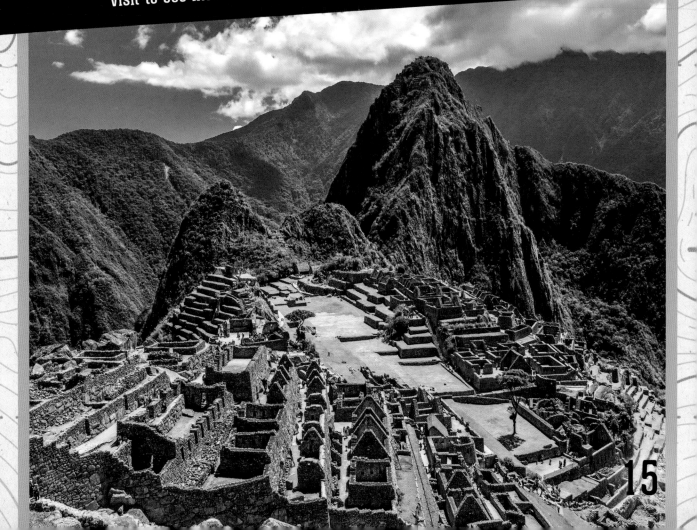

15

MEXICO CITY

Latin America, and Mexico in particular, is home to one of the oldest urban areas in the Western Hemisphere that has been continuously occupied by people—Mexico City. In the 1300s, the capital of the Aztec Empire, the ancient city of Tenochtitlán, stood in the same place where Mexico City stands today, but groups of people lived here even earlier than that. Centuries later, Mexico City is often ranked as one of the most populated cities in the world.

Major cities tend to be next to an ocean or river because it makes it easier to transport goods. Mexico City, however, is located away from the coast in a basin called the Valley of Mexico, which is surrounded by mountains.

CLOSE TO THE WATER—OR NOT?

The Valley of Mexico is also known as Anáhuac. This means "close to the water" in a language that was spoken by the Aztecs. But why was it called that if the area's not actually close to water? It turns out the valley once did have several lakes, but they've mostly dried up. In fact, the Aztec city of Tenochtitlán was built on an island in a lake. Over time, the Aztecs and Spanish drained the lake and built Mexico City there.

Mexico City's Metropolitan Cathedral is one of its most recognizable buildings. For years, it was sinking because it was built on land that had been a lake.

THINK LIKE A GEOGRAPHER

BEING LOCATED ON WHAT WAS ONCE A LAKE MEANS MUCH OF THE GROUND IN MEXICO CITY IS SOFT, WHICH CAN MAKE EARTHQUAKES IN THE AREA MUCH MORE DAMAGING.

Despite not being located on a major body of water, Mexico City's status as a major and populated city is likely due to its rich environment and long history. For centuries, people moved to the city because it was a place where jobs and opportunities were available. Before the Spanish came, people used rough trails to get to the city. These eventually became major roads used for trade routes, and finally paved the way for the transportation system in and around Mexico City today.

The Gulf of Mexico is located to the east of Mexico City, while the Pacific Ocean is to the west. The city's central location has helped it to become a common crossing point.

DIVERSITY AND DISCRIMINATION

Migration from all parts of the country, and many parts of the world, has led to a diverse population in Mexico City. Unfortunately, racial discrimination also happens here, and people with indigenous ancestry tend to live in lower-class, or poorer, areas of the city, while people of mostly European ancestry tend to live in the city's higher-class, or wealthier, areas. The conditions in these areas can be quite divided.

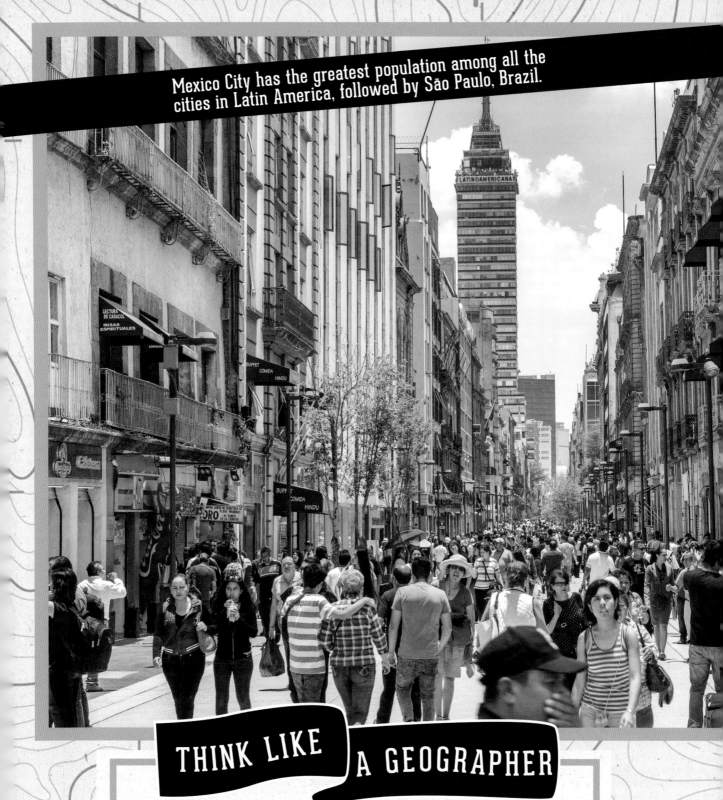

Mexico City has the greatest population among all the cities in Latin America, followed by São Paulo, Brazil.

THINK LIKE A GEOGRAPHER

MEXICO CITY HAS BEEN A CENTER FOR TRADE, POLITICS, AND CULTURE SINCE THE 13TH CENTURY. THE CITY IS RESPONSIBLE FOR AROUND A QUARTER OF THE MONEY BROUGHT INTO THE COUNTRY OF MEXICO.

THE RIO GRANDE

At about 1,900 miles (3,057.8 km) long, the Rio Grande is the fifth longest river in North America. It flows toward the Gulf of Mexico, creating the border between Texas and Mexico. Its most important tributary is the Conchos River in Mexico.

The Conchos provides water for nearby areas and is considered the main river system in the Mexican state of Chihuahua. Its water is used mainly for **irrigation** purposes, so it is vital for the state's agricultural industry. Nearby farmland is fertile, or able to support the growth of plants, but it is very arid, or dry. This means proper irrigation is needed in order for plants to grow and the area's agricultural industry to thrive.

HYDROELECTRICITY

Several hydroelectric plants line the Conchos River. Hydroelectricity is a form of renewable energy created by machines powered by moving water. It's commonly produced in power plants located in dams along rivers, such as the Boquilla Dam in the Conchos River. Moving water turns engines called turbines. This powers generators that turn the turbines' energy into electricity. While this is a valuable resource, man-made dams also restrict the natural flow of water, which can affect local animals. For example, dams can block fish migrations.

IRRIGATION: THE WATERING OF A DRY AREA BY MAN-MADE MEANS IN ORDER TO GROW PLANTS.

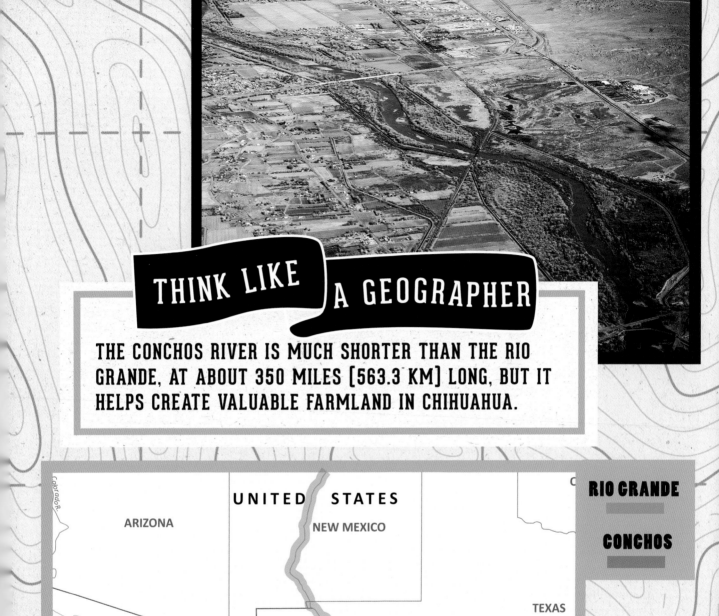

THINK LIKE A GEOGRAPHER

THE CONCHOS RIVER IS MUCH SHORTER THAN THE RIO GRANDE, AT ABOUT 350 MILES (563.3 KM) LONG, BUT IT HELPS CREATE VALUABLE FARMLAND IN CHIHUAHUA.

RIO GRANDE

CONCHOS

Colorado R.

UNITED STATES

ARIZONA

NEW MEXICO

TEXAS

SONORA

CHIHUAHUA

GULF OF CALIFORNIA

COAHUILA DE ZARAGOZA

MEXICO

BAJA CALIFORNIA SUR

SINALOA

NUEVO LEÓN

The Conchos River flows north toward the Rio Grande.
It provides about one-sixth of the Rio Grande's water.

THE GULF OF MEXICO

The Gulf of Mexico, which is bound by the United States to the north and Mexico to the west and south, is a body of water connected to the Atlantic Ocean that greatly influences the life and climate in parts of Latin America.

The Gulf of Mexico includes the continental shelf, a part of land under water that runs along the edge of a continent. This continental shelf is rich with fossil fuels, including petroleum oil and natural gas. These are valuable resources that people use to create energy. To gather them, governments and companies drill into the land at the bottom of the Gulf. Fossil fuels benefit the economy, but drilling can be harmful to the environment. Oil spills that happen because of drilling harm animals and other life, as well as beaches along the Gulf.

THINK LIKE A GEOGRAPHER

FOSSIL FUELS SUCH AS THE OIL AND GAS FOUND IN THE GULF OF MEXICO ARE NONRENEWABLE RESOURCES. HOWEVER, SOME SCIENTISTS BELIEVE THE GULF COULD PROVIDE GEOTHERMAL ENERGY, A RENEWABLE RESOURCE MADE FROM HEAT INSIDE THE EARTH.

NONRENEWABLE RESOURCE: A NATURAL RESOURCE THAT CANNOT BE REMADE OR REPLENISHED.

RENEWABLE RESOURCE: A NATURAL RESOURCE THAT CAN BE REPLENISHED NATURALLY.

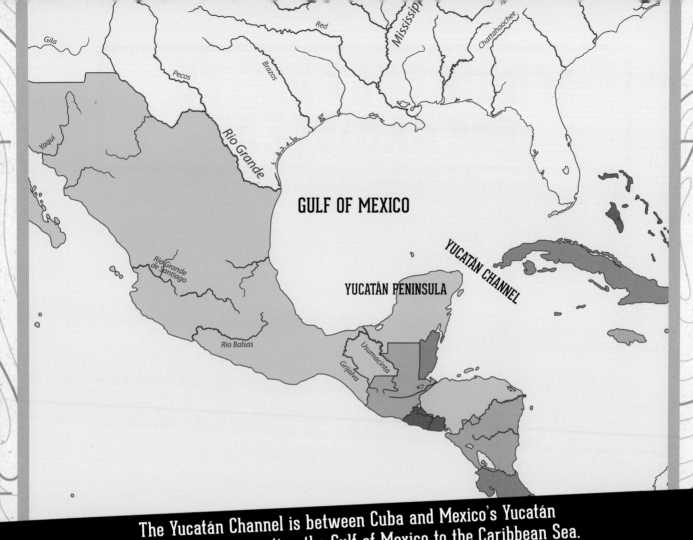

The Yucatán Channel is between Cuba and Mexico's Yucatán **Peninsula**, connecting the Gulf of Mexico to the Caribbean Sea.

CAN WE KEEP IT CLEAN?

Multiple rivers in the United States and Mexico flow into the Gulf of Mexico, draining water away from the land. Nearby farms in both countries often use chemicals to help crops grow and keep harmful plants and animals away. While these farms are helpful to the economy, the **runoff** from them often contains large amounts of these chemicals, which flow into and pollute the Gulf. This can harm organisms living in the Gulf, such as coral and mangroves.

FRuM THE GULF Tu THE CARIBBEAN

The Yucatán Peninsula is at the southeast end of the Gulf of Mexico. On the other side of the peninsula is the Caribbean Sea. Cancún, a city facing the Caribbean Sea on the peninsula, is a popular vacation spot for tourists due to its beaches and warm weather. Because of Cancún's appealing geography, it has been developed into a city with tall hotels and fancy resorts.

Caribbean coastal cities, such as Cancún in Mexico, Punta Cana in the Dominican Republic, and Bridgetown in Barbados, make a lot of money from tourism, helping their economies. The tourism industry is also full of jobs, and people tend to move to areas with a lot of jobs. Therefore, these areas have become home to those who work in the resorts.

HURRICANES

Hurricanes are storms that form in warm, moist air. This means the Gulf of Mexico and Caribbean Sea are prime locations for them to happen. As this warm air rises, pressure below decreases. More air moves in, warms, and rises. Then more air spins in again. Clouds form and the wind picks up to great speeds. Hurricanes are worst when over water. However, they move quickly and can seriously damage land, often **devastating** cities around the Caribbean and Gulf of Mexico.

THOUGH CANCÚN IS OFTEN THOUGHT TO BE AN IMPORTANT CITY THAT BRINGS IN MONEY, SOME NEIGHBORHOODS OUTSIDE THE RESORT AREAS ARE IN POOR CONDITION.

In 2005, Hurricane Wilma tore through the Caribbean and damaged much of Cancún.

KEEPING UP WITH CUBA

Cuba lies where the Atlantic Ocean, Gulf of Mexico, and Caribbean Sea all meet, about 90 miles (144.8 km) south of the United States and just south of the **Tropic of Cancer**. As an island, it has no bordering countries. The closest country is Haiti, which is 48 miles (77.2 km) east of Cuba in the Caribbean Sea.

During Christopher Columbus's 1492 journey, he claimed the island of Cuba for Spain. The land produced a lot of sugar, which became an important resource for the Spanish empire at the time. Spain ruled Cuba until the Spanish-American War in 1898, when U.S. and Cuban forces defeated Spanish forces. Soon, Cuba gained its independence and became its own country.

THINK LIKE A GEOGRAPHER

CUBA'S MAIN CITY AND CAPITAL IS HAVANA. ON THE NORTHWEST COAST, HAVANA ATTRACTS TOURISTS FROM ALL OVER THE WORLD AND IS KNOWN FOR ITS BEACHES.

TROPIC OF CANCER: THE NORTHERNMOST LATITUDE REACHED BY THE OVERHEAD SUN, WHICH IS PARALLEL OF THE LATITUDE AT 23.5 DEGREES NORTH OF THE EQUATOR.

SIZING UP THE ISLAND

The main island of Cuba is 777 miles [1,250.5 km] long. At its narrowest, it's only 19 miles [30.6 km] wide, but at its widest, it reaches 119 miles [191.5 km]. However, the country includes more than just this mainland. It's also made up of more than 1,000 smaller islands! If you put all these smaller islands together with the larger island, the total area of the country is still smaller than the state of Florida.

The temperature in Cuba usually stays between about 73°F [22.8°C] and 82°F [27.8°C] all year. However, it has a rainy season and hurricanes sometimes strike.

STUDYING THE LAND

Latin America is one of the most diverse geographical regions in the world. From the vast variety of plants and animals found in South America's Amazon Rain Forest to the supplies of copper and sodium nitrate found in the dry Atacama Desert, Latin America is a part of the world that provides us with many resources and offers endless opportunities for discovery and learning.

The geography of Latin America, from the rolling green Maya Mountains in Central America to the vast **pampas** of central Argentina, affects the climate of the region, and has the power to impact many parts of the world—even outside of Latin America itself. By studying the natural features of the land, geographers have been able to make discoveries that can help people and countries around the world.

TO THE EXTREME

Latin America is often considered an area of extremes. This means its geography, climate, and other features come in very wide varieties and areas not too far away from each other can be very different from each other. For example, one city in Colombia gets nearly 290 inches [736.6 cm] of rain per year, while some areas in northern Chile have no record of ever having rain!

PAMPA: AN EXTENSIVE, GENERALLY GRASS-COVERED PLAIN OF TEMPERATE SOUTH AMERICA EAST OF THE ANDES.

THINK LIKE A GEOGRAPHER

FROM HURRICANES TO VOLCANIC ERUPTIONS TO EARTHQUAKES, AREAS OF LATIN AMERICA ALSO DEAL WITH EXTREME NATURAL DISASTERS. THE VALDIVIA EARTHQUAKE OF 1960 IN CHILE WAS THE STRONGEST EARTHQUAKE EVER RECORDED.

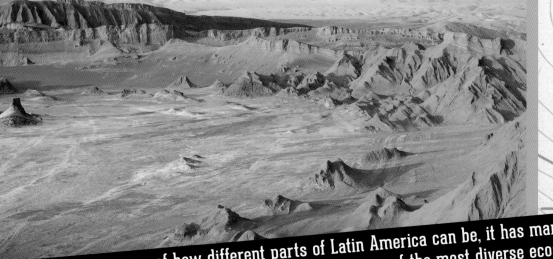

Because of how different parts of Latin America can be, it has many different biomes. The Amazon Rain Forest has one of the most diverse ecosystems in the world, while the Atacama Desert supports very few life-forms.

BIOME: A NATURAL COMMUNITY OF PLANTS AND ANIMALS, SUCH AS A FOREST OR DESERT.

GLOSSARY

altitude: Height above sea level.

arable: Good for farming.

climate change: Long-term change in Earth's climate, caused primarily by human activities such as burning oil and natural gas.

devastate: To cause widespread damage.

fossil fuel: Matter formed over millions of years from plant and animal remains that is burned for power.

peninsula: A piece of land that is connected to a mainland and is surrounded on three sides by water.

runoff: Water, often from rain, that flows over the surface of the ground into other bodies of water.

savanna: A grassland with scattered patches of trees.

significant: Large enough to have an effect.

terrain: The type of land in an area.

thrive: To succeed or do well.

tributary: A small river or stream that flows into a large body of water.

FOR MORE INFORMATION

BOOKS

Brooks, Susie. *Brazil.* London, UK: Wayland Publishing, 2017.

Fabiny, Sarah. *Where Is the Amazon?* New York, NY: Grosset & Dunlap, 2016.

Shea, Therese M. *The Land and Climate of Latin America.* New York, NY: Britannica Educational Publishing, 2018.

WEBSITES

Biodiversity of the Amazon
www.nationalgeographic.org/maps/biodiversity-amazon/
View a map and learn more about the Amazon—an important part of Latin America's geography—on this website.

Central America and the Caribbean
www.ducksters.com/geography/centralamerica.php
Learn more about Central America and the Caribbean, and check out maps of the region!

South America: Physical Geography
www.nationalgeographic.org/encyclopedia/south-america-physical-geography/
Find out more about South America's geography here.

INDEX